WHEN IS A PLANET NOT A PLANET?

THE STORY OF PLUTO

ELAINE SCOTT

SCHOLASTIC INC.
New York Toronto London Auckland Sydney
Mexico City New Delhi Hong Kong Buenos Aires

ACKNOWLEDGMENTS

Many people were very helpful as I worked on this book. In particular, I want to thank Antoinette Beiser, librarian at the Lowell Observatory, Dr. Mike Brown at the California Institute of Technology (Caltech), Jane Platt from the Jet Propulsion Laboratory (JPL), and Stephen Tellier of the Lunar and Planetary Institute for their patience with me and my questions.

ISBN-13: 978-0-545-11599-5
ISBN-10: 0-545-11599-X

12 11 10 9 8 7 6 5 4 3 2 1   8 9 10 11 12 13/0

Printed in the U.S.A.   08

First Scholastic printing, October 2008

The text was set in 16-point Sabon.

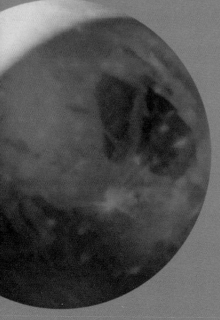

PHOTO CREDITS

Courtesy NASA/JPL-Caltech: 2, 22 • Peter Arnold, Inc./Alamy: 4 • Agence Images/Alamy: 6 • Visual Arts Library (London)/Alamy: 7, 11 • Paul Almasy/CORBIS: 8 • Gustavo Tomsich/CORBIS: 9 • North Wind Picture Archives/Alamy: 10, 12 • Lunar and Planetary Institute: 16–17 (all planets) • Courtesy NASA/JPL-Caltech: 18 (Uranus), 19 (Neptune) • The Print Collector/Alamy: 18 (Herschel) • NASA, ESA, J. Parker (Southwest Research Institute), P. Thomas (Cornell University), L. McFadden (University of Maryland, College Park), and M. Mutchler and Z. Levay (STScI): 18 (Ceres) • Osservatorio Astronomico di Palermo: 18 (Piazzi) • Deutsches Museum: 19 (Galle) • NASA/JPL: 19 (asteroids) • NASA, ESA, and G. Bacon (STscI): 20 (Pluto) • The Lowell Observatory: 20 (Lowell, Tombaugh) • C. R. O'Dell (Rice University) and NASA: 24 • Michelle Gengaro-Kokmen: 25, 26 • Dr. R. Albrecht, ESA/ ESO Space Telescope European Coordinating Facility/NASA: 27 • Dan Durda, Fellow, International Association of Astronomical Artists: 28 • California Institute of Technology: 30 • Palomar Observatory, California Institute of Technology: 31 • Mark Garlick (Space-art): 32 • International Astronomical Union: 34 • NASA/JPL-Caltech/T. Pyle (SSC/Caltech): 35 • NASA: 37

6. WHAT IS A PLANET?

Because scientists always check and recheck their work, Mike Brown and his team of astronomers didn't announce their discovery of Eris until January 5, 2005, after they had had a chance to verify their information. When they revealed their discovery, many people thought the solar system had gained its tenth planet. But others disagreed. Soon an argument was raging among astronomers all over the world. And the argument came down to one question. What, exactly, is a planet?

It seems surprising, but until August 24, 2006, science had never had a definition for the word "planet." Dictionaries had definitions, of course, but most said something similar to "A large celestial body that circles around the Sun or another star." For a scientist, that definition had problems. For one thing, what is meant by "large body"? Jupiter, the largest planet in our solar system, is 88,700 miles in diameter, and it is a planet. Pluto is only 1,440 miles in diameter and—at the time—it was a planet, too. The question "What is a planet?" needed an answer, and the International Astronomical Union decided to create not one definition but three.

The IAU came up with three classes of objects that orbit the Sun: planets, dwarf planets, and small solar-system bodies.

The IAU decided that a celestial body is a planet if it:

1. orbits the Sun
2. is round or nearly round, because its gravity has pulled it into that shape
3. is big enough and has enough gravity to "clear the neighborhood" around its orbit

The first two qualifications for planethood, orbiting the Sun and a round shape, are easy to understand. The concept of "clearing the neighborhood" is a little more difficult.

The Planet Definition Committee.
Top row, from left:
Dr. Andre Brahic, France;
Dr. Iwan Williams, England;
Dr. Junichi Watanabe, Japan;
Dr. Richard Binzel, USA;
bottom row, from left:
Dr. Catherine Cesarsky, president-elect of the IAU;
Dava Sobel, author;
Dr. Owen Gingerich, USA.

asteroid: a small rocky object in the solar system that orbits the Sun. Asteroids are too small, and travel too fast, to be considered planets.

astronomer: someone who engages in the study of astronomy.

astronomy: the study of stars, planets, and other celestial bodies outside Earth's atmosphere.

celestial body: a naturally occurring object visible in the sky.

comet: a celestial body made of frozen dust and gas; comets often form long, bright tails.

dwarf planet: a celestial body that orbits the Sun and is not a moon or satellite of another planet. Unlike planets, a dwarf planet is not large enough to clear its orbit of other objects.

energy: the ability to do work; the ability to cause matter to move or change.

gas giant: a large planet, such as Jupiter, that is composed mostly of gaseous elements.

gravity: the force of attraction all bodies or masses in the universe possess; the larger the body, the more gravity it has.

helium: a gas that is lighter than air.

hydrogen: a light gas that burns easily; the most abundant element in the universe.

hypothesis: a proposed scientific explanation based on observation.

International Astronomical Union (IAU): an international group of astronomical societies that has the authority to name stars, planets, asteroids, and other celestial bodies.

law: in science, a general statement that describes regularly repeating facts or events.

matter: any substance in the universe that takes up space; matter can be liquid, solid, or gas.

Milky Way: the galaxy that is home to Earth's solar system.

moon: a natural satellite of a planet.

nuclear reaction: any reaction that involves a change in the nucleus of an atom, which is the smallest part of matter.

observatory: a building or location outfitted with telescopes and other equipment for watching celestial bodies.

orbit: the curved path one object takes as it revolves around another.

orbital plane: the imaginary plane in space on which all the planets orbit.

physics: the science that studies how matter is affected by energy.

planet: a large round celestial body that occupies its own orbit around a star.

protoplanetary disk: a disk of dust and gas that orbits a new star.

satellite: an object that orbits another object in space; satellites can be man-made or natural.

solar system: a star and the collection of celestial bodies that orbit it.

star: a celestial body that creates its own light by nuclear reaction.

telescope: an instrument that uses lenses, mirrors, and sometimes cameras to make distant objects appear larger and closer.

terrestrial planet: a planet having a rocky surface; Earth is a terrestrial planet.

theory: a statement based on a confirmed hypothesis.

universe: all existing things, including all matter and all energy, on Earth and in space.

FOR ADDITIONAL READING

BOOKS

Croswell, Ken. *Ten Worlds: Everything That Orbits the Sun*. Honesdale, Pa.: Boyds Mills, 2006.

Fleisher, Paul. *The Big Bang*. Minneapolis: Twenty-First Century Books, 2005.

Orr, Tamra. *The Telescope*. New York: Franklin Watts, 2005.

Steele, Philip. *Galileo: The Genius Who Faced the Inquisition*. Washington, D.C.: National Geographic, 2005.

Taylor-Butler, Christine. *Pluto*. New York: Children's Press, 2005.

Thomson, Sarah L. *Extreme Stars! Q&A*. New York: HarperCollins, 2006.

Wright, Kenneth. *Scholastic Atlas of Space*. New York: Scholastic, 2005.

WEBSITES OF INTEREST

National Aeronautics and Space Administration
http://www.nasa.gov
Explore the universe and learn about the latest discoveries.

New Horizons
http://pluto.jhuapl.edu
Launched on January 16, 2006, New Horizons is the first mission to Pluto and is scheduled to arrive at the edge of our solar system in 2015. The site includes mission information as well as educational materials for teachers and students.

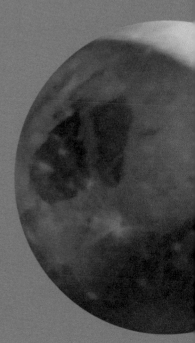

Welcome to the Planets

http://pds.jpl.nasa.gov/planets/welcome/pluto.htm

The Jet Propulsion Laboratory of the California Institute of Technology hosts a collection of many of the best images from NASA's planetary exploration program with extensive annotations.

Star Child: A Learning Center for Young Astronomers

http://starchild.gsfc.nasa.gov/docs/StarChild/StarChild.html

The Astrophysics Science Division of NASA provides an interactive site, divided into two age-appropriate levels, offering information and educational activities related to space, astronomy, and the solar system.

Amazing Space

http://amazing-space.stsci.edu

Designed primarily for educators but available to everyone, this site offers answers to cosmic questions, homework help, images, and online explorations that encourage learning through interactive programs.

Home page of Michael E. Brown, Division of Geological and Planetary Sciences, California Institute of Technology

http://www.gps.caltech.edu/~mbrown

An informative and entertaining page that includes Mike's story of finding Eris and his reaction to Pluto's demotion.

Note: Page numbers in **bold** type refer to illustrations.